FEMALE SPORTS
STARS

CHELSEA HOUSE PUBLISHERS

SUPERSTARS OF WOMEN'S TENNIS

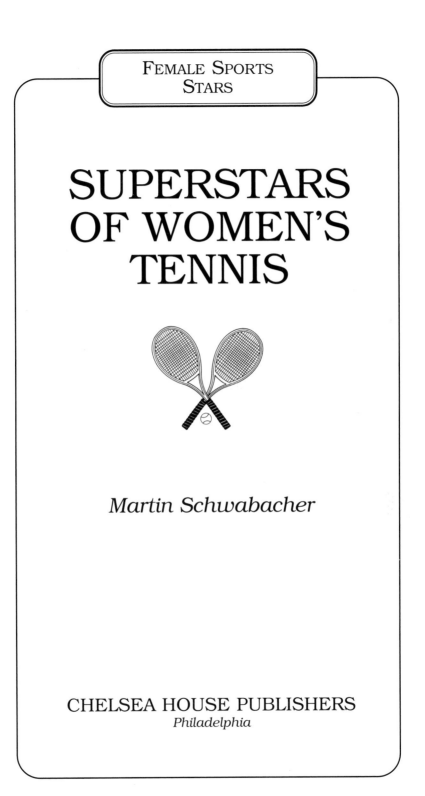

Martin Schwabacher

CHELSEA HOUSE PUBLISHERS
Philadelphia

CHELSEA HOUSE PUBLISHERS

Produced by Daniel Bial Agency and Associates
New York, New York

Senior Designer   Cambraia Magalhães
Picture Research   Sandy Jones
Cover Illustration   Bill Vann
Frontispiece photo   Martina Navratilova

First Printing
1 3 5 7 9 8 6 4 2

Library of Congress Cataloguing-in-Publication Data

Schwabacher, Martin.
        Superstars of women's tennis/ Martin Schwabacher.
            p.   cm.—(Female sports stars)
        Includes bibiliographical references (p.) and index.
        ISBN 0-7910-4393-2 (Hard)
            1. Women tennis players—Biography—Juvenile literature.
[1. Tennis players. 2. Women—Biography.] I. Title. II. Series.
GV994.A1S43   1997
796.342'092'2—dc20
[B]   96-36689
                                                                             CIP
                                                                             AC

CONTENTS

INTRODUCTION

F rench-born Suzanne Lenglen was tennis's first great female star. She won at Wimbledon in 1919 and then repeated the feat the next three years. Kathleen McKane broke her streak in 1924, but Lenglen won again in 1925. The French star was never invited back to Wimbledon after she turned pro in 1926, but the $50,000 she received for her first tour—a phenomenal sum of money in those days—must have eased her pain.

Helen Wills Moody was the next great player. She won four years in a row at Wimbledon (1927-1930) and added triumphs in 1932, 1933, 1935, and 1938. Moody also won seven times at the U.S. Open.

Stars in the 1940s included Alice Marble, Pauline Betz, Sarah Palfrey Cooke, and Margaret Osbourne. The 1950s was blessed with the immense talents of Maureen ("Mo") Connolly, Maria Bueno, and Althea Gibson. In 1957 and 1958, Gibson, the first black tennis star, won back-to-back championships at both the U.S. Open and Wimbledon.

Margaret Court Smith dominated women's tennis in the early 1960s, winning a grand slam—titles in the Australian, French, Wimbledon, and U.S. Opens—all in one year. But Smith would be upstaged soon by a terrific teenager, one who would change how women's tennis was played—and its popularity.

Billie Jean King played with a vigor and tenacity that women's tennis had not seen before. She wanted to win and didn't care if everyone knew it. Some said she "played like a man," and eventually she did play a man, Bobby Riggs, who had won singles titles at both Wimbledon and the U.S. Open. When King crushed the older Riggs, she gave women's tennis a boost that it still feels today.

After Billie Jean King, women's tennis has enjoyed an even greater group of stars. The personalities of these women range tremendously. King was a wild and outgoing character, while Chris Evert tended to be shy and demure. Martina Navratilova is gregarious, whereas Steffi Graf has a solid personality. Monica Seles is unpredictable and controversial.

Women's tennis has produced stars from all over the globe. Navratilova was born in Czechoslovakia, Graf in Germany, Seles in Yugoslavia. In addition, stars have come from England (e.g., Virginia Wade), Australia (Evonne Goolagong), Spain (Arantxa Sanchez Vicario and Conchita Martinez), Argentina (Gabriela Sabatini), Russia (Natalia Zvereva), Bulgaria (the Maleeva sisters), Japan (Kimiko Date), and Switzerland (Martina Hingis). Players of great potential are also coming from such countries as Israel, Indonesia, Cambodia, China, and Croatia.

Naturally, many Americans are also competing at the highest levels. Current stars include Lindsay Davenport, Mary Pierce, Mary Jo Fernandez, and Chanda Rubin.

The great champions described in this book are very different. But their stories all share one thing: each player pushed herself to the limit and worked as hard as she possibly could to be her best. Their achievements have inspired thousands of girls around the world. Somewhere, at this very minute, a girl is playing tennis who may turn out to be the greatest champion of them all.

1

BILLIE JEAN KING

No one has done more for women's tennis than Billie Jean King. On the court, she was a ball of fire. Though she was not a particularly smooth or graceful player, she dominated matches with her quickness, strength, intelligence, and will to win.

King displayed her lively, forceful personality in her tennis. She played a daring, aggressive style known as "serve and volley." Instead of playing it safe by waiting at the baseline for her opponent to make a mistake, she rushed the net at every opportunity, swatting the ball out of the air before it could hit the ground. Off the court, she was just as intense—if not more so. Always outspoken and unafraid of making waves, King fought to bring women the same respect, fame, and prize money as the male players earned. When the big tourna-

In 1961, Billie Jean King (then known as Billie Jean Moffitt) teamed with Karen Hantze (left) to win the doubles title at Wimbledon. The unseeded duo beat the first-, third-, and fouth-seeded teams to win the trophy.

ments treated women unfairly, she helped create new tournaments just for women. She cajoled other top players to split with the dominant United States Lawn Tennis Association (USLTA) and join her on the women's tour. In the first year of the women's tour, she won 19 tournaments, becoming the first woman to take in more than $100,000 in prize money in a single year. Her exploits made the upstart tour a hit, ensuring that women would never again be taken for granted by the USLTA.

King was born Billie Jean Moffitt on November 22, 1943, in Long Beach, California. She grew up in a happy, middle-class family. Her father was a firefighter, and her mother stayed home to care for her family, as women were expected to do at that time.

Like millions of American children, Billie Jean loved baseball. She was a good player, starring on a local softball team with girls much older than she was and playing shortstop with the men at firefighters' picnics. If there had been a professional women's league to aim for, she might have become a major leaguer like her brother, Randy Moffitt, who became a star relief pitcher with the San Francisco Giants. Even as a young girl, Billie Jean knew she wanted to be the best at something. If there was no future in baseball, she would find another sport where there were no limits for women. Tennis was considered an acceptable sport for girls, so at age 11 she saved eight dollars from mowing lawns and bought herself a racquet.

Billie Jean soon became the Southern California champion in her age group. But while being a girl was not a problem in tennis, she discovered that money was. Most tennis players came from wealthy families that could

afford clothes, rackets, lessons, and travel expenses. As a 12-year-old, Billie Jean had once been barred from a tournament group photo because she didn't have a tennis dress like all the other girls. Two years later, she won a chance to go to the national juniors championship in Ohio, but she couldn't afford the plane ticket. Two local clubs chipped in $350, but even so, she and her mother had to take a train. It was Billie Jean's first time on a clay court, which favors a slower backcourt game, and she lost in the quarterfinals. Afterwards, most of the contestants moved on to another tournament. Out of travel money, Billie Jean returned home—more determined than ever.

In addition to her money problems, she did not have the ideal body for tennis. She tended to put on weight, gaining 25 pounds once in a single summer by eating too much ice cream. Though she loved to rush the net, she had a hard time reaching some of the shots her oppo-

Billie Jean King's style was not the smoothest, but no one had greater determination.

King enters the Houston Astrodome in 1973 to play Bobby Riggs in the most heavily hyped tennis match ever. However, King was all business when she routed the self-admitted "male chauvinist pig."

nents tried to whack past her because she was short. She also had terrible vision and had to wear glasses because her eyes were too flat to wear contact lenses.

But Billie Jean was a dynamo on the court, and the chunky, funny-looking kid with short hair and glasses quickly attracted attention, earning the nickname Little Miss Moffitt. In 1961, on her very first trip to Wimbledon—the world's most important tournament, held each year in England—Billie Jean and her doubles partner, Karen Hantze, upset several highly ranked teams and grabbed the doubles championship, beating Margaret Court Smith and Jan Lehane in the finals. Billie Jean was only 17 years old. The next year, she played Smith, the tournament's top-seeded player, in the first round of the singles tournament. In a stunning upset, the teenager knocked off the champion. It was the first time in history a number-one seed had been eliminated from the tournament in her opening match.

But Billie Jean was not yet good enough to make it past the quarterfinals. The following year, 1963, Billie Jean reached the Wimbledon finals, but this time Smith whipped her for the championship. It was a painful loss; Billie Jean said that "for years afterwards, whenever I needed something to psyche me up before going out to play, I tried to remember the feelings I had during that match, and the sense of utter desolation and failure. . . . I didn't want to repeat it—ever."

Smith encouraged the youngster, pointing out that she simply didn't play enough. Billie Jean loved the game, but she did not yet think of it as a career. At the time, she thought it was more important to go to college, get married, and start a family.

Today, tennis is a lucrative profession, and some parents push their kids into it. But as King later wrote in her autobiography, *Billie Jean*, "at the time I was growing up, who in their right mind would have pushed their daughter into tennis? There wasn't a nickel in it, and you were literally called a bum if you stayed in it long enough to be any good. Some reward."

Since tennis players now rack up millions of dollars in prize money and endorsements, this may be hard to believe. But in the 1960s, what Billie Jean said was absolutely true. The most important tournaments, including Wimbledon, did not even accept professional players. Tennis existed mostly as an "amateur" sport, officially played not for money but for the love of it. In reality, this meant that the game appealed mostly to the wealthy.

If Billie Jean Moffitt had met and married a different sort of man, she quite possibly would have retired from tennis and become a homemaker. But she was fortunate in her choice of a fiancé. Her boyfriend, Larry King, was not at all threatened by having a successful athlete for a wife. He urged her to put her dreams first and keep striving to be number one. He even encouraged her to accept an offer to train for three months in Australia, even though it meant they would be apart.

In Australia, one of the world's top coaches, Merv Rose, helped Billie Jean make some fundamental changes in her game. She learned a new way to serve and to hit a forehand shot. It took a lot of hard work just to become as good as she had been before, but the new style, once she mastered it, gave her the tools to beat anybody in the world.

In 1965, Billie Jean and Larry were married. Again, she thought of quitting tennis so that she could cook and clean for him. But Larry refused, reminding her, "You have the potential to be the best in the world."

In 1966, her dream of winning a Wimbledon singles title at last came true. She vanquished her old nemesis, Smith, in the semifinals and defeated three-time Wimbledon champion Maria Bueno for the championship.

Over the next ten years, Billie Jean won the Wimbledon singles tournament six times. She also continued to compete in both doubles and mixed doubles (in which each team is made up of one man and one woman). During her career, she won four mixed doubles championships and a whopping ten women's doubles titles at Wimbledon. Her grand total of twenty Wimbledon championships is still the all-time record for men or women.

In October 1967, Wimbledon followed the lead of other tournaments by allowing both pros and amateurs to compete. King promptly turned pro and joined the National Tennis League. She and nine other men and women traveled across Europe, performing in makeshift courts and high school gyms. She made very little money, and the league quickly folded, but King liked the hard grind of the touring pro.

Back in America, King joined the USLTA tour, which ran the country's biggest tournaments. But she was outraged that the men's prize money was routinely five or six times greater than the women's. The men running the big tournaments ignored the women's complaints.

Billie Jean urged Gladys Heldman, who ran *World Tennis* magazine, to start a competing tournament just for women. The USLTA leaders were furious. They suspended all the women who played in the upstart tournament from the USLTA. Undaunted, the rebels created an entire tour that competed directly with USLTA events. The prizes were bigger, and the new tour featured the added attraction of America's best female player—Billie Jean King—at almost every event.

Many women players were afraid to buck the powerful USLTA. But Billie Jean would have none of it. She argued loud and long, urging the other women to be strong and stand up for their rights. She also

Billie Jean King had the greatest impact of anyone on women's tennis. At Wimbledon in 1979, she takes a break with some other stars who shared in her legacy: from left to right Rosie Casals, Chris Evert, Martina Navratilova, and Tracy Austin.

played her heart out on the tennis court with the goal of becoming the first woman to win $100,000 in a single year—not just for the money, but to win respect for women athletes and make the public take them seriously. She succeeded, winning $117,000 in 1971, the new tour's very first year.

To further advance the cause of the women players, King urged tennis players from around the world to join a new union, the Women's Tennis Association. In 1973, she became its first president. United into a powerful force by their union, the women demanded that tournaments treat them fairly—or they would not play. The threat of mass boycotts convinced the tournament managers that they could no longer take advantage of female players, and they agreed to pay the women at least 80% of what the men earned. Her fearless leadership made Billie Jean King an example not just for her fellow tennis players but for all women.

That same year, the eyes of the world focused on women's tennis when Billie Jean King accepted a challenge from former Wimbledon champion and self-proclaimed male chauvinist Bobby Riggs to play a match for $100,000 in the Houston Astrodome. Riggs was 55 years old, but he had already beaten King's long-time rival Margaret Court Smith in a similar match he called "the Mother's Day Massacre." King was angry that Smith had fallen for Riggs's tricky shots, and she set out to avenge Smith's loss for the pride of women everywhere.

As the match grew nearer, the whole country was abuzz. King was challenging long-held prejudices about the supposed inferiority of women. Everybody had an opinion, and many people—husbands and wives, even congressmen and congresswomen—were betting on the outcome. Major magazines did cover stories about the showdown, and Riggs was constantly on television, making wisecracks about King and women in general.

The pressure on Billie Jean was tremendous. But she did not mind pressure; in fact, she thrived on it. With the eyes of the world on her, she confidently drove to the net just as she always did, running Riggs ragged with a dazzling array of powerful, accurate shots. It was Riggs who cracked first, double faulting on the final point of the first set. King took command of the match, winning decisively in three straight sets.

When it was over, a crowd gathered around Billie Jean. Before a mass of cameras and reporters, King was asked what winning the match meant to her. "Maybe it means that people will start to respect women athletes more," she answered. "But it's not just me. There are many more to take my place. And in the next decade, I think you'll see women athletes finally getting the attention they've deserved all along."

She was right. In the following years, women's tennis exploded in popularity, and her goal of moving coverage of women's tennis off the women's pages and onto the sports pages came true. Billie Jean King had helped bring respect not just to women's tennis but to women in general. "People are starting to look up to us now," she said proudly in 1973. "We've made it okay for a girl to say, 'If I enjoy playing tennis and sweating, I don't care what my boyfriend thinks."

King retired from active play in 1984.

2

CHRIS EVERT

In the early 1970s, the explosion of interest in women's tennis created by Billie Jean King received a boost from an unexpected source. Seemingly out of nowhere, a 16-year-old girl from Florida named Chrissie Evert began beating established pros in tournament after tournament. She quickly became known as America's Sweetheart, and her immense popularity raised interest in women's tennis to unprecedented heights.

On the surface, Chris Evert and Billie Jean King could not have been more different. King was a volatile player who talked to herself on the court, interacted with the crowd, and thrived on her strong emotions. Evert was quiet, restrained, and polite, showing no emotion while she played. While King was a daring, attacking player who liked to rush the net

In 1974, 19-year-old Chris Evert won Wimbledon—after already winning the South African, French, and Italian Open championships that year. Prince Philip handed her the trophy for winning Wimbledon.

and force the action, Evert preferred to stay back, patiently returning every shot until her opponent made a mistake. King dazzled with an array of attacking shots of all spins and speeds, while Evert relied on accuracy and consistency. One writer said of Evert, "Playing her is like playing a wall; the ball comes back, inevitably, incessantly." King dominated matches with her legendary will to win and killer instinct. Evert's quiet intensity was just as intimidating; she never smiled, never looked nervous, and rarely made an error. The contrast in their styles created a classic rivalry that fans found irresistible.

Christine Marie Evert was born on December 21, 1954, in Fort Lauderdale, Florida. She was the second of five children, all of whom learned to play tennis at an early age. Chris's father, Jimmy Evert, managed the Holiday Park Tennis Center, the largest tennis complex in Florida, where he also worked as a teaching pro. With the help of their father's coaching, all the Evert children became good players. Chris's brother's John and Drew achieved high rankings in Florida, and her sister, Jeanne, was a nationally ranked junior player who eventually played professionally. But creating professional tennis players had never been the Everts' goal; tennis was just something that the whole family could do together.

Chris was a shy child. Her mother said of Chris, "At home she is a peacemaker. She could never bear fights among the children. Whenever there was trouble, she never got excited. Quietly, she tried to stop it." Her calm, steady personality fit the conservative style of tennis she played and gave her the patience to practice hour after hour, every day.

She played for 2 1/2 hours every day after school, and more on weekends. She was not a natural athlete, but through hard work and practice, she learned to hit the ball exactly where she wanted. Unlike most champions, Chris had no great passion for the game as a child. "I had no feeling for the game," she admitted. "I just did it because my dad brought me over to the courts. It was his idea. I didn't dislike it, I mean, it was something to do. When you're eight or nine you don't really have many hobbies."

A player who knew Chris growing up in Florida, Sue Sapp, said, "Chris was never really young. She always had a mature head on her shoulders." Since she had been practicing seriously from the age of six under the supervision of a professional coach, by age 15 Chris was good enough to compete against adults. But even in their wildest dreams no one predicted that her career would take off as fast as it did.

She first grabbed the world's attention in 1970, when she was just 15 years old, by beating Margaret Court Smith. Smith had dominated the other players so thoroughly that year that she had won all four of the major championships—Wimbledon and the Australian, French, and U.S. Open titles—a "Grand Slam" achieved by only one other woman in history,

Chris Evert was famous for her two-handed backhand.

Maureen "Little Mo" Connolly. Evert followed this upset over Smith with wins over such top players as Virginia Wade and Billie Jean King. By the time she entered the U.S. Open in September 1971, she had won more than 40 matches in a row.

Even before the tournament started, the blonde, blue-eyed teenager had become a sensation. At a time when much of the public was still not comfortable with the idea of women as athletes, the cute girl called "Chrissie" was very unthreatening. She wore makeup and ribbons in her hair during matches and did not challenge traditional ideas about femininity. In fact, she approved of them, saying "It's important to look feminine. . . . I want to be known as a woman, not just a tennis player." Many

When Chris Evert and Jimmy Connors each won the singles title at Wimbledon in 1974, they were engaged to be married. Evert broke off the relationship before the wedding took place.

older players who had fought hard to create the opportunities Chris now enjoyed resented that Evert showed no appreciation of their struggles for equality. Those who strove to show they could play as hard as men did were offended when she made such comments as, "no point is worth falling down for." But Billie Jean King defended Evert, saying it could only help their cause to have a star so beloved by the public. "Chris is great for women's tennis," she said. "This is a 16-year-old kid who's beating the best people in the game. It's beautiful."

From the first round of the tournament, young Chrissie Evert was the center of attention. Fans flocked to see her play. In a break from tradition, all of her matches were scheduled on the stadium's center court. Her first match, a 6-1, 6-0 victory over the German Edda Buding, drew 9,000 spectators—three times the number for other matches. In her second-round match, her opponent, Mary Ann Eisel, won the first set, took the lead in the second set, and was one point from victory six times. But Evert held her off to win the second set in a tie breaker, then stormed back to win the third set 6-1. The *New Yorker* magazine reported, "Evert left the court to a roaring ovation. She had captured the imagination of the spectators as no other young American player had in years."

Two more come-from-behind victories put her in the semifinals for a showdown against Billie Jean King. It was the match everyone had been waiting for. Not only was it a battle between top players of two different generations, it was a classic clash between the attacking style of King and the backcourt style of Evert.

But there was much more was at stake for King than there was for Evert, who was thrilled just to get that far in her first U.S. Open. King was fighting for the future of the Virginia Slims tour, which was then in its first year. If the tour's best player could not defeat a 16-year-old, it would lose credibility. As King put it, "A monster had been created and I had to put an end to it." Using her powerful serve and assortment of spins and speeds, King trounced the newcomer, salvaging the pride of the women's league.

When Evert joined the Slims tour in 1973, she was perceived as unfriendly and was not popular with the other players. Still only 17, Chris traveled with her mother. She had never been outgoing, and some people mistook her reserve for arrogance; one player even called her a "spoiled brat." It was hard for some not to resent her quick success. Upon turning professional at age 18, for example, Evert immediately signed a contract that paid her $50,000 to endorse a line of tennis dresses. While most players brought four or five dresses to tournaments, Evert traveled with 20 different outfits, each with matching hair ribbons. Years later, Evert recalled, "I'd never been one of the girls. When I was younger, I was too shy to go out and seek their friendship. I realize now that if I'd been a little more open, I wouldn't have felt as uncomfortable around other players."

On the court, Chris turned her unemotional exterior into one of her biggest weapons. She believed that her intense concentration and self-discipline gave her an edge over the other players. Her icy calm, she once said, "keeps them guessing." The 1977 Wimbledon champion Virginia Wade wholeheartedly agreed that

Evert was the most consistent performer ever in women's tennis. Here she reaches for a forehand in the 1986 U.S. Open.

Evert's mental toughness gave her an advantage: "Chris's mind on the court was definitely the strongest out of all the great champions I've played. Even stronger than Billie Jean because it was much more stable. I've seen Billie Jean playing lots of bad matches. . . . I almost never saw Chris playing a bad match."

The only tournament that seemed to unsettle Evert was Wimbledon. Unlike in America, the fans and press were not kind to her in Britain. Even in the United States, she was sometimes referred to as "Little Miss Cool" or the "Ice Princess." But in England, her emotional reserve on the tennis court earned her the nickname "Ice Dolly," after a frozen dessert popular there.

It was at Wimbledon in 1973, however, that she fell in love with another young American tennis star, Jimmy Connors. Connors was not popular in England either, but for very different reasons. While Chris was perceived as cold and remote, Jimmy was cocky, brash, and prone to emotional outbursts that the British considered vulgar and rude. Chris was attracted to Jimmy because his freewheeling, unrepressed personality helped relax her and draw her out.

The romance between the tennis stars was big news. Interest in Evert's private life increased even more in late 1973 when the couple announced that they were engaged. They set a wedding date for November 8, 1974.

For Chris Evert, Wimbledon in 1974 was like a fairy tale. Although Wimbledon is played on grass, a fast surface that favored an attacking style, Evert had been working hard to develop a more complete game. She had greatly improved her serve, which was the weakest part of her game, and she had learned to rush the net now and then. Margaret Smith was absent from Wimbledon that year, as well as two other Wimbledon champions who had eliminated Evert in previous years: Billie Jean King and the young Australian Evonne Goolagong lost in the early rounds. Evert soared all the way to the finals, where she beat Olga Morozova 6-0, 6-4 for the championship. At 19, she was the youngest winner since 1952, when 17-year-old Maureen Connolly won the first of three straight titles. The day after Evert conquered Wimbledon, Jimmy Connors won the men's title.

As their wedding drew near, the two realized they were not ready to marry. They were both very young, and neither wanted to stop playing tennis. Chris explained, "I don't know when we could have seen each other. We will be on the road, playing different circuits. We realize how foolish it would be for us to go through with the wedding at this time. We might have looked back and said to ourselves, 'why didn't we wait?'" In January 1975, two weeks after her 20th birthday, Chris announced the engagement was off.

No longer traveling with her mother or engaged to Connors, Chris became much more independent and self-confident and made friends among the other women on the pro tour. One of the first whom she opened up to was Billie Jean King. "Billie Jean is so independent, I could listen to her for hours," Chris said of her new friend. Talking to King, she said, helped her "start to question the things I've been brought up on." But King refused to take credit for the changes in Evert, saying, "Chris is no dummy. She's very intelligent. She's had three or four years to live her life in different environments, to meet different people, to see different situations. She's had to learn for herself." In 1976, her fellow players showed their respect for Chris by electing her president of their union, the Women's Tennis Association.

In 1975, Evert again found romance at Wimbledon when she met British player John Lloyd. The couple married four years later, but the marriage ended in divorce, and Evert eventually married Andy Mill, a one-time top skier, with whom she has two children.

Evert, the first player ever to win 1,000 matches, retired in 1989 after 19 years as a pro.

3

MARTINA NAVRATILOVA

The person who finally dethroned Chris Evert as the queen of women's tennis was a powerful serve-and-volley player named Martina Navratilova (pronounced Mar-TEE-na Na-VRAH-ta-low-VAH). Though she was just two years younger than Evert, Martina's journey took many years of ups and downs and twists and turns before she reached the top.

Born Martina Subertova on October 18, 1956, in Prague, Czechoslovakia, Martina grew up in an athletic family. Her grandmother had been a tennis champion who at her peak was ranked number two in Czechoslovakia. Martina's mother, Jana Subertova, was a top skier who gave lessons for a living, and her father, Miroslav Subert, was a ski patrolman.

Martina Navratilova started to make a name for herself at a young age, but she lacked discipline on and off the court. Here she competes at the Virginia Slims Tournament at age 17.

After they married, they lived in a ski lodge named Martinovka, which means Martin's place. Martina was named after this cozy lodge.

When Martina was three, her parents divorced. She and her mother moved into a one-room home overlooking a tennis court in the town of Revnice. Martina learned to ski almost as soon as she could walk, and as she grew older she became devoted to other sports, including soccer and hockey. When the ski season ended, her mother enjoyed playing tennis, especially with the man who gave tennis lessons and maintained the courts, Mirek Navratil. Mirek was warm and friendly, and Martina had no objection when he and Jana decided to marry. In Czechoslovakia, wives and daughters add the ending "-ova" to the husband's last name, so Martina Subertova became Martina Navratilova.

By age six, Martina was eager to play tennis like her parents. At first, she hit a ball by herself off a wall, but soon her stepfather took her out on the court and taught her to play. "The moment I stepped onto that crunchy red clay, felt the grit under my sneakers, felt the joy of smacking a ball over the net, I knew I was in the right place," Martina remembers. Mirek taught a conservative, baseline game well suited to the clay court. But from the beginning, Martina preferred the attacking style of Billie Jean King. She remembers that "even as a little kid, I'd totter up to the net."

Martina became so devoted to tennis that she played from the time the snow melted in the spring until the snow fell again the next winter. Because there were no indoor courts in Revnice, she had no place to play during the long winter. The nearest indoor court was 16 miles away in Prague. By age nine, Martina's progress was so impressive that her father took her to Prague for a tryout with George Parma, a former tennis champion who was now a coach with the Czech Tennis Federation. After Parma watched the small, wiry athlete dash around the court for a half hour, he said, "I think I can do something with her." From then on, Martina took the train to Prague once a week for lessons.

Martina liked her new coach right away. His calm, focused style was a perfect match for her emotional, impulsive nature. Parma taught her new techniques, such as a one-handed backhand, which gave her more range than the two-handed backhand she had been using. He also taught her strategies to use against other players.

Martina began traveling to other cities to play in tournaments. At age 12, she was allowed to go to West Germany, where she beat several much older players.

Traveling to West Germany was a rare experience in communist-controlled Eastern Europe, which was separated from the West by a heavily patrolled border known as the Iron Curtain. The government had taken away many basic freedoms, including the right to leave the country. In 1968, the Soviet Union crushed a Czech freedom movement with a military invasion. Martina helplessly threw rocks at the Soviet tanks as

After Navratilova defeated Chris Evert at the finals of Wimbledon in 1978, she still got a big hug. Earlier she had called her first victory over Evert "the happiest day of my life."

Navratilova stretches for a volley at the net. She proved to be the greatest serve-and-volley player in women's tennis history.

they rolled through her town. "There were hundreds of cars and tanks and soldiers," she remembers. "It was unreal." Tens of thousands of demoralized Czechs, including George Parma, gave up hope and emigrated to the West.

Even without Parma, the Czech Tennis Federation had a strong training program. Tennis players were allowed to compete in tournaments outside of the country to win pride for the country and prize money for the federation. By 1972, the skinny little girl from Revnice was already the Czech national champion, and at age 16, she was allowed to go to the United States for two months.

Martina was bubbly, cheerful, and wildly enthusiastic about everything American. She picked up English quickly—it was her fourth language—and learned American slang from the TV and radio. She loved the big American cars and colorful clothing, but most of all, she loved American food—especially junk food. She stuffed herself with hamburgers, and her appetite at breakfast earned her the nickname "pancake champ." As a skinny girl in Czechoslovakia, she had been known as "Prut," which means "Stick." But nobody was calling her that anymore; in just eight weeks in America, she gained 25 pounds.

The young Czech was immediately popular with the American players and fans. They liked her daring, aggressive serve-and-volley style, and she was a good sport, correcting errors by umpires even if it cost her the point. Though she was quick, strong, and very talented, she tired easily and her emotions sometimes got the best of her, which kept her from beating more disciplined players such as Chris Evert.

Still, she did extremely well for a 16-year-old, and in 1974 she returned to America. After this stint, she was ranked number 10 in the world and was named rookie of the year. Her prize money went to the Czech Tennis Federation to help other young players, but Martina saved enough of her expense money to buy her parents a car—a Czech Skoda—so they could travel throughout Eastern Europe to see her play.

Martina wanted nothing more than to go back to America for the 1975 season, but the Czech government was worried that she was becoming too "Americanized." Ignoring her Czech chaperones, she hung around with American players, and each time she returned home, she was more critical of her own country. But Martina was now among the world's best players, and the government finally agreed to give her another chance to win glory for her country.

The 1975 season was her best yet. She beat top contenders such as Virginia Wade, Evonne Goolagong, and Margaret Smith and reached the finals of the French, Italian, and Australian Opens. She called her first victory over Chris Evert "the happiest day of my life." When Martina beat Chris again a few weeks later, Evert invited her to become her doubles partner. Together they won four tournaments in 1975, including the French Open. Martina's earnings for the year totaled $200,000, and this time—after hiring an American business agent—she kept 80% of the money for herself.

Martina became more and more smitten with the American lifestyle, and the Czech federation confronted her about rumors that she planned to renounce her Czech citizenship and defect to the United States. She denied the rumors, but the truth was, she was tempted. "I didn't want to defect, not totally," she said later. "I just wanted to play tennis." But the Czech government was so concerned they told Martina she could not go to the U.S. Open. They eventually relented but told her she had to return as soon as the tournament was over.

In New York, Martina faced a tough decision. If she defected, she might never be able to go home again. But if she returned to Czechoslovakia, she said, "I had no idea when I would get out again." Her whole future hung in the balance. "I was a wreck," she remembers. "But once I was here, I knew I wasn't going to go back."

Martina moved into a friend's house in Beverly Hills, California, and began the process of becoming an American citizen. "It was the first time in my life when I didn't have to get permission to do anything," she remembered. "It all hit me at once. I went wild." She went on spending sprees, using her prize money to buy clothes, furs, jewelry, and five cars. Her eating habits were also out of control—she amazed the other players by eating a quart of ice cream at one sitting, followed by an entire large pizza. She no longer worked hard in practice, and her lack of conditioning made her fall apart in long matches.

Though Martina was a better natural athlete than the other players, including the reigning champ, Chris Evert, her lack of focus and discipline kept her from playing as well as she should have. Mentally, she could not keep up with Evert; if she made a mistake, she would get upset and yell at herself, and if she made several mistakes, it would disrupt her play for the entire match. In her first 11 months as an American, Navratilova did not win a single tournament. "All the freedom almost killed my tennis," she said. Her low point came during the 1976 U.S. Open, when she lost to Janet Newberry in the first round. After the match, Martina began weeping so hard that Newberry had to help her off the court.

Martina knew she needed help with the mental aspect of her game. She received it from her friend Sandra Haynie, a professional golfer. Like Evert, Haynie was composed and professional during matches. She helped Navratilova develop the discipline she needed for the long hours of training required to play her best.

After two years of hard work, Martina improved so much that she was challenging Evert for the top ranking. She reached number one when she won the 1978 French Open and then beat Evert in the Wimbledon finals, her first Wimbledon title. Up until then, Chris had won 23 of 29 matches against Martina. Navratilova proved the victory was no fluke in 1979 by winning 5 of 7 matches against Chris, including Wimbledon, solidifying her hold on the top spot in the rankings.

Off the court, Martina fell in love with famous author Rita Mae Brown. Rita Mae encouraged Martina to learn more about the cities they visited on the tennis tour. Now, instead of hanging around the court playing cards or reading magazines, Martina went out every day to visit a museum or see a play or concert. Eventually, Martina and Rita Mae moved into a house together.

Living with an outspoken gay-rights advocate meant that Martina had to put up with the hostility and ignorance of people who were intolerant of homosexuality. But having given up so much to come to America so that she could be free to live how she chose, Martina was not going to back down now. Though she broke up with Brown a year later, her pride and strength made Navratilova a hero in the gay-rights movement as well as on the tennis court.

In 1979, Martina's father, mother, and sister moved to the United States. But her parents were not happy in America. They had no jobs and few friends, and they were uncomfortable being supported by their daughter. After a few months, they moved back to Czechoslovakia, where Martina bought them a beautiful house. But she could not return home to see it. "I wish I could drop in for a visit," she said longingly.

In 1980, Martina's ranking slipped to number three. Partly because of all the distractions in her personal life, Martina was practicing barely 90 minutes a day, and she admitted, "I just hit the ball in my head some days." She still had the talent, but had lost her stamina and self-discipline. It bothered her that she was wasting her potential.

"I always got away with so much. But you can't get by anymore. The players are too good," Martina said. She vowed to let nothing get in the way of her training and to see how good she could become. This time, she brought in basketball star Nancy Lieberman to help her

work out. Navratilova began practicing tennis for three hours each day, as well as running sprints, lifting weights, and doing all sorts of drills and exercises. She cut down on high-fat foods such as meat and ice cream and hired a nutritionist to tell her what foods would keep her in top physical condition. Next, she hired a former tennis pro, Renee Richards, to improve her strategy and tactics. Richards helped her develop an even more powerful serve and a top-spin backhand. But more important, she taught her to carefully study her opponents' strengths and weaknesses. "Renee would tell me about my opponent's personality, her tendencies on court, so I could be ready for her when we played."

Navratilova became so much better than everybody else that she won 90 of her 93 matches in 1982, winning 15 out of 18 tournaments and reclaiming the number-one ranking

Navratilova had her greatest successes at Wimbledon, where she won six singles titles in a row. In 1983, she showed off the trophies she received for winning in singles and doubles.

from Evert. Martina no longer would be known as a happy-go-lucky player ruled by her emotions. She was now surrounded by a team of professionals working to bring every aspect of her game to peak performance level.

Her most satisfying win that year was her victory over Evert in the U.S. Open. Despite her success, the one title that had always eluded her was the championship of her new country's own tournament. In 1981, she had beaten Evert in the semifinals but lost to Tracy Austin in the finals. The crowd had cheered her, knowing how much she loved America and how badly she wanted the title, and their support had moved Martina so much that she cried. But it was not until the 1982 Open that her dream came true. She was relentless throughout the tournament, averaging only 52 minutes to eliminate each opponent and beating Evert 6-1, 6-3 in the final. Out of a total of 103 games throughout the tournament, Navratilova lost only 19. The old, inconsistent Navratilova was history. She was so dominant that she became the first female player to earn over $6 million in a single year.

In 1983, Navratilova got even better. She won 16 of 17 tournaments, including her fourth Wimbledon, and for the year she won 86 of her 87 matches. One reporter asked, "Do you think you're just too good for the women?" Martina answered, "I hope so. I want to make it as boring as I can." But she believed that the other women could also make great improvements if they trained the way she did. Martina's doubles partner, Pam Shriver, with whom she won four straight Wimbledon titles from 1981 to 1984, predicted, "Martina's overall fitness program will change the way women play tennis forever."

Martina's string of victories had reached 54 when she lost in January 1984 to Hana Mandlikova, a young Czech who had once been her ball girl back home. But instead of losing her focus, Navratilova immediately went on to win her next 74 matches in a row, the longest winning streak in the history of women's tennis. She was one win away from sweeping all four Grand Slam events in 1984 when she lost the Australian Open to another Czech, Helena Sukova. Many argued that Navratilova had already achieved a historic Grand Slam sweep by winning the four tournaments in succession between 1984 and 1985, but others argued that it was not a true Grand Slam because the streak spanned two calendar years.

Martina's hard work and mental toughness had turned her into the best player of the 1980s. In 1991, at the age of 35, she matched Chris Evert's career record of 157 tournament championships, making her the winningest female player of all time. One of Navratilova's proudest achievements is her sterling record at Wimbledon, where she just seemed to get better and better with age. Though King's titles in doubles and mixed doubles make her the greatest all-around winner at Wimbledon, Navratilova now holds the all-time record in singles play with a whopping nine Wimbledon championships, including a record six in a row.

In the 1990s, the fall of communism in Eastern Europe meant that Martina could at last return home to visit her family and friends. But while Czechoslovakia is where Navratilova was born, America is the place where she grew up, and she will always consider it her home.

4

STEFFI GRAF

Chris Evert's stunning success from age 16 and her immense popularity during her long reign caused thousands of young girls to flock to tennis courts. She had set the precedent for girls playing world-class tennis while still in their teens, and her fame, glamour, and riches made her one of the most recognizable women in America. Many tennis-playing parents began eyeing their young progeny to see if they had the talent to play professionally, and girls began to enter tournaments at younger and younger ages.

By far the most successful of these young girls was Steffi Graf. Though she alarmed many by turning pro at the astonishing age of 13, she turned out to be not only the best of the new young players but also one of the best

Steffi Graf serving at the 1988 U.S. Open. The 19-year-old German won the tournament to complete her Grand Slam—victories at the Australian, French, Wimbledon and U.S. Opens all in the same year.

players in history. Steffi's father was very
involved in her training from the very beginning. But what set her apart from the rest of
the new generation—aside from her awesome
talent—was the total devotion she had to the
sport. While the parents of many young girls
prod them to practice more and more, the
greatest challenge Steffi's father faced was getting her off the tennis court.

Stephanie Maria Graf was born June 14,
1969, in Mannheim, Germany. Her parents,
Peter and Heidi Graf, both played tennis at a
local club where her father was the top-ranked
player. As a toddler, Steffi would sit and watch
them play. By the time she was three, Steffi
wanted to play, too. Though she was not even
big enough to hold a racket, every day she would
plead, "Please play with me, Papa."

Finally, Peter gave in. He sawed the handle off an old racket and gave it to her. For a
net, he tied a string between two chairs in the
living room. Soon Steffi could hit the ball
back and forth. They broke so many lamps in
the living room that they moved their
games to the basement, where a couch served
as the net.

Steffi's father told her that if she returned
the ball 10 times in a row, he would give her a
breadstick. For a string of 15, he promised her
a cola. When that became too easy, the challenge became 25 in a row, for which Steffi was
rewarded with ice cream and strawberries.

She played so intently that even the tele-
phone ringing could not make her take her eyes
off the ball. At age five, Steffi moved outdoors
to a real court, where she quickly beat all the
local eight-year-olds. At age six, she won her
first tournament.

Peter marveled at his daughter's single-minded pursuit of tennis. "Unlike the other children," her father remembers, "she did not hit the ball and then look all around at other things. She was always watching the ball until it was not in play anymore."

When Steffi was eight, her father sold his car dealership and his insurance business so he could become a full-time tennis coach. The family moved from Mannheim to the nearby town of Bruhl, where Peter opened the Graf Tennis Club. The Grafs now had six courts right next to their house, and Peter began coaching Steffi every day after school.

When Steffi was 12 years old, she won the German championship for girls age 18 and under. She then won the 12-and-under championship for all of Europe. That year, she was ranked number 12 among West German adults. In the fall of 1982, four months after she turned 13, she became a professional tennis player by beginning her career ranked number 214 in the world.

Although she was only in the eighth grade, Steffi quit school and began traveling on the pro tour. She continued to study with the help of a tutor, but tennis was now her job. For some children, this would have been a hard and lonely life, but for Steffi, it was a dream come true.

Steffi didn't win any tournaments her first year, but she did advance to the quarterfinals of a tournament in England and the semifinals of an event in Germany. But by 1985, Steffi had moved up to number 22 in the world. She cruised to the finals of several professional tournaments, including the German Open.

At the U.S. Open that year, Graf played the greatest match of her career thus far. In the quarterfinals, she faced the third-ranked player in the world, Pam Shriver. That day the temperature reached 100 degrees, but neither player gave in to the heat. The first set had to be decided in a tie breaker, which Graf won. When the second set also reached 6-6, Shriver won the tie breaker. In the third set, the two players again fought to a 6-6 tie. Graf went on to win this third tie breaker and take the match 7-6, 6-7, 7-6.

It was a historic contest. Tie breakers are always tense and exciting, but this was the first women's match ever to require three tie breakers in a row. In the grueling heat, the players battled for 2 hours and 45 minutes.

Though she was thrilled to make the final four, Graf was crushed in the semifinals by Martina Navratilova, who was still the dominant player in the world.

Later in 1985, Graf lost again to Navratilova in the finals of a tournament in Florida. Instead of joining the postgame ceremony, she ran off the court. Many people criticized her poor sportsmanship and questioned whether her father was right to allow her to quit school. Some even felt he was pushing her too hard. In fact, Steffi explained, "My father makes sure I do not play too much."

Steffi's forehand was already one of the best in the world. No one could hit the ball harder from the right side. By learning to put more topspin on her backhand like she did on her forehand, Steffi's game became strong enough to challenge anyone.

When she returned to tournament play in 1986, Steffi immediately proved that she was

Graf's game combines the consistency of Chris Evert with the strength of Martina Navratilova. No other tennis player has been ranked number one longer than Steffi Graf.

now one of the best players in the world. She outslugged the 31-year-old champion Chris Evert 6-4, 7-5 in the finals of the Family Circle Magazine Cup in South Carolina for her first major tournament title.

After years of domination by Evert and Navratilova, women's tennis now had a new contender for the top spot. By the end of 1986, Graf had moved up to number three, behind only the two great champions.

When 1987 began, it was clear that Steffi's apprenticeship was over. In March, she swept all the way through the Lipton Players Championship without losing a set. Graf beat

Navratilova easily, 6-3, 6-2. Afterward, Martina said, "There's no two ways about it, she out-played me. Today she was the best player in the world." Graf's final victim, Evert, fell even more swiftly, losing 6-1, 6-2.

Just 17 years old, Steffi was now considered the player to beat. Heading into the French Open, she had won six straight tournaments and was unbeaten for the year. "I used to be a little bit scared of Chris and Martina," she declared. "Now it's their turn to be afraid of me."

But Martina was still ranked number one. When the two faced off in the French Open final, each took a set 6-4. Martina surged ahead in the final set and was one point from victory when she double faulted. On a second match point, this time with Graf ahead, Navratilova again missed two straight serves, and Graf had her first Grand Slam title. Steffi also made history as the youngest player ever to win the French Open.

Graf's victory set up a dramatic showdown with Navratilova at Wimbledon. Martina had won the tournament the past five years in a row. But Navratilova was now 30 years old and knew she could not overpower the younger, stronger Graf. So she decided to outsmart her. Keeping the ball away from Graf's cannonlike forehand, Martina served to Steffi's backhand the entire match. Navratilova's greater experi-ence neutralized Steffi's power, and Martina held off the frustrated Graf for a 7-5, 6-3 victo-ry. Martina had won a record sixth straight Wimbledon title.

No one else was able to stop Graf, however, and she whipped player after player with machine-like precision in her pursuit of num-ber one. In August, Steffi finally seized the top spot in the rankings. During the entire year, Steffi lost only twice, but those two losses were crucial, as they came to Martina in the finals of two Grand Slam events. Steffi was clearly the number one player that year, but Martina was still champion of Wimbledon and the U.S. Open. Many people—including Navratilova—felt that Steffi had not yet proven she was better than Martina. To do that, she had to win the big ones.

Steffi responded to the doubters like a true champion. In 1988, she had one of the greatest years anyone has had in the history of tennis. She won the first Grand Slam event of the year by beating Chris Evert in the finals of the Australian Open. In the French Open she became the first woman since 1911 to win the championship without letting her opponent win a single game, taking just 32 minutes to dispatch Natalia Zvereva 6-0, 6-0 in the finals.

As Wimbledon approached, Graf looked so dominant that people began to believe she might win all four Grand Slam events in a single year. This is the biggest achievement a tennis player dreams of. Only four people—Don Budge, Rod Laver, Maureen Connolly, and Margaret Court—had ever done it. As great as King, Navratilova, and Evert were, none of them had won the entire Grand Slam in a single year.

Steffi knew that to beat Martina at Wimbledon she had to improve her backhand serve return, the shot Martina had exploited to beat her at Wimbledon the previous year. Because Martina was left-handed, her serve was extremely difficult to return from the left side. To prepare for Martina, Steffi spent four months practicing with a left-handed male tennis pro.

*Graf holds the Rosewater
dish after winning her
sixth Wimbledon title
in 1995.*

As expected, Graf and Navratilova met in the finals. Steffi jumped to a 5-3 lead, but then Martina rattled off six straight games, winning the first set and jumping ahead in the second. Graf's preparation paid off. She then broke Martina's serve seven straight times and won 12 of the last 13 games. Her 5-7, 6-2, 6-1 victory left no doubt that Steffi was the better player.

Only one Grand Slam event remained: the U.S. Open. She breezed through her competition and reached the final once again. Opposite the net stood Gabriela Sabatini, the Argentine star who had beaten her twice earlier in the year. After splitting the first two sets, Graf overpowered Sabatini in the third for a 6-3, 3-6, 6-1 victory. After the final shot, Steffi threw her racket in the air and ran to the stands to hug her father, mother, and brother. In the award ceremony, she received her $275,000 winner's check and a gold bracelet with four diamonds on it—one for each Grand Slam event. Though she was happy and excited, Steffi said that mainly "It's a relief. Now I've done it. There's no more pressure. Now, there's nothing else that people can tell me I have to do." Just 19 years old, Steffi had earned a permanent place in tennis history.

By the time Steffi lost again, her winning streak had reached 46 consecutive matches. In 1989 and 1990, she remained so dominant that over an 11-month period she won 66 matches in a row, the second longest winning streak in modern history. She set an all-time record by holding onto the number-one ranking for 186 weeks in a row, from August 17, 1987 to March 10, 1991. She won three straight Wimbledon titles from 1991 to 1993, and three out of four Grand Slam events in 1993, reinforcing that she is one of the all-time greats. By the time she won the U.S. Open in 1996, just about everyone was willing to admit that Graf was the greatest of all time.

Graf's biggest problem in the 1990s came from a surprising source: her father. She had always relied on him to handle all of her finances, just as he had handled so many other aspects of her career. But to the horror of everyone in Germany, where Steffi is a national hero, it was revealed that Peter Graf had not been paying income taxes on much of Steffi's earnings. Her winnings and endorsement fees totaled millions of dollars, but in some years, he had not filed any taxes at all, a serious crime for which he was jailed.

Still, nothing could diminish Steffi's achievements. Steffi's reign at the top of women's tennis had not been seriously challenged until the emergence of another young European player, Monica Seles. Their rivalry would form the main story in women's tennis in the early 1990s.

5

MONICA SELES

$\mathbf{M}$any people considered the late 1980s a rather boring time for women's tennis. The reigning champion, Steffi Graf, had no serious challenger, and though her down-to-earth personality was likable enough, her simple, family-oriented lifestyle created no excitement. For fans of women's tennis, the arrival of Monica Seles could not have come at a better time. Not only did her incredible talent rocket her to Graf's level in almost no time, but her unpredictable and sometimes outrageous behavior gave the newspaper columnists plenty to talk about. Sadly, Seles is probably best known for being assaulted by a deranged man during a tennis match. But before that, she won millions of fans with her kooky, irrepressible enthusiasm, Woody Woodpecker giggle, hyena-like oncourt grunting, and a fearsome combination of two-fisted forehand and backhand

At age 17, Monica Seles became the youngest player ever to win the Australian Open.

shots that Chris Evert once likened to "Steffi's forehand off both sides."

Monica Seles (pronounced Mo-NEE-ca SELL-esh) was born December 2, 1973, in Yugoslavia. Her father, Karolj, a former triple-jump champion, worked as a professional cartoonist and documentary filmmaker, and her mother, Esther, as a computer programmer. Her father gave her a tennis racket when she was six, but she quit after a few weeks. Her interest was rekindled when her brother, Zoltan, brought home a trophy from the national junior championships.

Karolj ensured that she maintained her interest in tennis by drawing Tom and Jerry cartoons on her tennis balls and putting stuffed animals on court, which she got to keep if she hit them with the ball. He taught her to grip the racket with two hands even from the forehand side, which allowed her to hit the ball much harder than other girls her size. At the age of 8, she won a major tournament even though "she couldn't keep score and had no idea when the match was over," Zoltan reported.

The tiny girl quickly racked up title after title. By age 9, she was her country's champion in the 12-and-under age group. She won the 12-and-under European championships at age 10, and the 14-and-under title at age 12. When she was still 12 years old, she became the youngest person to be named Yugoslavia's Sportswoman of the Year.

During a tournament in Florida, she was spotted by tennis coach Nick Bollettieri. "I saw this little pipsqueak, and she was beating the heck out of everyone," Bollettieri remembers. "I was so impressed that I offered Monica a full scholarship and invited the entire family to come and live at the academy. She was all feet and could barely see over the net, but could she play!"

In 1986, the family moved to Florida. At Karolj's suggestion, Monica went two years without playing any tournaments or practice matches. "Everyone wanted her to play junior tournaments, but it wasn't the best thing," Karolj said. Monica agreed, explaining, "Taking the pressure off helped me develop more. I could work on all kinds of new things and never worry about winning or losing."

It was certainly not a lack of competitiveness that kept her out of tournaments. In fact, no one else at the academy wanted to practice with her because she hit every ball to win. Another student, future men's number one player Jim Courier, remembers that when no girls would play with her, "Nick ordered me to hit with Monica one day. First ball, whap!, she smacks a winner. Next, whap!, winner. I said, 'O.K., I'm impressed. You can play. Now let's practice.' Uh-uh. Whap, whap, whap! After 15 minutes I walked off. I told Nick, never again."

After honing her skills for two years, Seles made her major tournament debut in 1987, and by 1989 she had won her first Virginia Slims tournament, beating Chris Evert in the final. Still just 15, she attracted attention at the French Open by making it to the semifinals before falling to Graf. By reaching the quarterfinals in 8 of 10 tournaments, she

Seles hits the ball harder than anyone else in women's tennis. She's also known for her loud grunts as she pounds the ball.

raised her ranking from 86 to 6 by the end of the year.

But in early 1990, Monica fell into a slump. She injured her shoulder, prompting criticism that she was putting her young body through too much strain by competing against top professionals. "If she were my daughter," Navratilova remarked, "I'd say, 'You're staying home, you're staying in school.'" She also was struggling through a growth spurt that caused her to shoot up nearly six inches, from about 5'3" to 5'9", in just 16 months. "Sometimes I felt dizzy from growing so much," she reported. Her new height forced her to relearn her game. "All of a sudden I was seeing the court at different angles. And before, I didn't have to bend my knees to hit the ball." Eventually, her new height made her tougher than ever. As Navratilova put it, "A year ago I was looking down at her; this year I'm looking up at her. And it's ticking me off."

That same spring, the Seleses caused controversy by leaving Bollettieri's academy and claiming that Karolj had been Monica's true coach. By March, Monica was winning tournaments again. On May 13 she routed Navratilova 6-1, 6-1 for the Italian Open championship. Navratilova said, "It was like being run over by a truck." A week later, Seles whipped Graf 6-4, 6-3 for the German Open title, ending Graf's 66 match winning streak. Seles went into finals of the French Open riding her own streak of 31 straight wins. Beating Graf 7-6, 6-4 for the title, the 16-year-old Seles became the youngest woman ever to win the French Open and the youngest winner of a Grand Slam tournament since 1887.

Seles was beginning to threaten the top players in the game. Arantxa Sanchez Vicario said, "She thinks she can win every match and every tournament. The other players are afraid of her." In November 1990, Seles passed Navratilova in the rankings to reach number two, which left her trailing only Graf, who had been perched at number one for 3 1/2 years.

On March 11, 1991, Seles ended Graf's record 186-week run at the top of rankings. In addition to being the youngest winner of the French Open and the Australian Open, Monica was now the youngest women ever to be ranked number one in the world. She was just 17 years old.

The vivacious teenager was having more fun than ever off the court as well. She became known for constantly changing her hair style and color, from straight dark brown to frizzed corn yellow to a golden-henna-colored short wave. She considered shaving her head bald like the singer Sinead O'Connor, until "somebody reminded me my head would get pretty sunburned." Seles also enjoyed posing for photo layouts in fashion magazines such as *Elle* and *Vogue.* Ted Tinling, a top designer of tennis dresses for decades, thought Seles's passion for fashion was just what women's tennis needed. "Monica is the one," he exclaimed. "Thank God Almighty, glamour has finally returned to the game."

Monica became a student of tennis history, often quoting from Billie Jean King's book *We Have Come a Long Way.* She cited as her inspiration the legendary champion from the 1920 Suzanne Lenglen, whose stylish outfits received as much attention as her five straight Wimbledon titles. Chris Evert complimented her respect for tennis's traditions, saying, "Monica's the first one of the new breed to show

In 1993, a Steffi Graf fan stabbed Seles in the back during a change-over. The injury kept her out of the game for over two years.

the responsibility to the game a top player should have. . . . She has such self-assurance and poise for someone her age." But others found her public image contrived and called her "publicity hungry."

Even her defenders did not contest that she was usually hungry when it came to food, especially butter. She spread mounds of butter across steak, french fries, even pizza. "Ugh. Gross, totally grody, I know," she said. "But I can't help it. I must be addicted to butter. I just can't eat any food without it. . . . I know I've got to switch my diet habits. But I'm waiting until after Wimbledon. If I quit cold on butter now,

I'm afraid it would be too much of a shock to my system."

Her penchant for publicity reached new heights in 1991 at Wimbledon. Just three days before play began, she announced that because of a "minor accident," she was withdrawing from the tournament. To make matters worse, she dropped completely out of sight, refusing to meet with members of the WTA or the press to explain the situation. Her disappearance fueled wild rumors about her health and speculation that she was pregnant. Instead of setting the matter straight, she continued to dodge the press for the next 27 days. She finally surfaced at a huge press conference that *Sports Illustrated* called the "silliest performance of the year by a major athlete." Seles said she had not been able to clarify her medical condition because she had received four different diagnoses from different doctors, and "I myself was totally confused." She claimed that she was unaware of the controversy she had caused, even though she had been photographed wearing a disguise.

Though she was just a teenage girl trying to have fun, Seles was humbled somewhat by the ridicule she received for her antics. She explained, "I learned when you are Number One, how much weight our words have. . . . You can't just blurt words out." The storm of publicity didn't hurt her wallet, however. By the end of 1991, she had earned $2.45 million in prizes, a single-season record. Her endorsement contracts with Yonex, Canon, Fila, Perrier, and Matrix pushed her earnings over $7 million, making her the 12th-highest-paid athlete in the world, male or female. She had won every Grand Slam she entered that year, along with seven other tournaments.

In 1992, she solidified her hold on the number-one ranking. She dropped only one set in winning the Australian Open, which gave her 4 of last 5 Grand Slam titles. Her toughest, most grueling tournament of the year was the French Open. In the fourth round, she fell behind 4-1 in the final set to Akiko Kijimuta, but ran off five straight games to win. In the semifinals, she trailed Gabriella Sabatini 4-2 in the final set before gutting out the victory. She faced Graf in the finals, and they fought to a 6-6 tie in the third set. Since it was the final set of the tournament, no tiebreaker was used; play would continue until one player took a two-game lead. Seles ultimately triumphed, taking the final set 10-8. She said afterward it was "the hardest I've ever had to work for a Grand Slam title."

As the 1992 Wimbledon grew near, the press frenzy that always surrounded her reached a fever pitch. Because of her controversial disappearance the year before, the always rude English tabloids prepared to pick on her mercilessly. This time, they zeroed in on her notorious grunting, which even her friend Ted Tinling had once compared to the sound of a goose being strangled. One tabloid staged a phone-in contest, offering a prize to the person who could best imitate her loud shrieks. Another measured the volume of Seles's grunts with a decibel meter, concluding that the readings were comparable to those for a locomotive. The players criticized her cries, too, saying they were unduly distracting. During one match, Navratilova complained to the officials, "She sounds like a stuck pig!"

Monica apologized, saying, "It's part of my game. I hate it, I can't help it." Clamping down on herself in the finals against Graf, she managed to silence her grunting, but it appeared to affect her play as she fell listlessly to Steffi, 6-2, 6-1.

Upset by the taunting, Seles took a month off after Wimbledon, but she was in top form again by September, when she captured the U.S. Open title without losing a set during the entire tournament. She started 1993 well, winning the Australian Open for the third straight year. But then a viral infection caused her to miss 63 days of action, the longest rest ever by a number-one player.

But soon she would endure a far longer and more serious absence from the game. In April 30, 1993, Seles was playing in a small tournament in Hamburg, Germany, when Gunter Parche, an unemployed lathe operator from East Germany, walked up behind her chair. With no warning, he pulled out a knife and stabbed her in the back. The wound was only half an inch deep, but emotionally, the damage was profound.

The attacker told the police that he wanted to clear the way for his fellow-German Steffi Graf to regain the number-one ranking. To Monica's great disappointment, the other players refused to freeze her ranking during her absence, and her attacker's wish came true when Graf became the new number one. Even more disturbing to Seles was that after Parche was convicted of the attack, he received only a two-year suspended sentence and was released. "The guy who attacked me got what he wanted, and he was let out, free,"

When Monica Seles finally returned to tennis in 1995, she was as good as ever—and possibly even better. She defeated Martina Navratilova in an exhibition match, barely lost to Steffi Graf in the U.S. Open finals, and then won her fourth consecutive Australian Open.

Seles said. "I think anybody in my situation could have a big problem with that."

Even after she recovered from her wound, the emotional trauma caused by the attack prevented her from returning to the courts. After discussing the situation with Monica, Billie Jean King said, "She doesn't know if she'll ever be able to get over the fear and come back again." In a rare interview, Seles remarked, "The one place I felt safe was a tennis court—and that was taken away from me." She suffered from recurring nightmares and saw a therapist who treated her for post-traumatic stress disorder. She withdrew from public life, receiving comfort from her family and a support group for crime victims. "There were and are people I can call if I wake up at 2 in the morning and have a problem," she said. "And now there are people who can call me if they want. They aren't celebrities, or anything like that, just people who share one thing—having been stabbed. And they really helped me to deal with my situation."

It took 27 months before Seles was able to play again in public, in an exhibition match against Martina Navratilova on July 29, 1995. Led by Navratilova, a group of players convinced the WTA to let Seles share the number-one ranking with Graf. Her first official tournament was in Toronto, and she won it handily. But it was in the 1995 U.S. Open that Seles proved she was herself again. She made it all the way to the finals before losing a tough three-set match to Graf. But just as important, she proved she was ready to have fun again, painting her fingernails all different colors and attending two Broadway shows and a New York

Giants game while she was in New York for the tournament.

A series of minor injuries kept her from competing regularly, but by January 1996, she was ready for the next Grand Slam tournament, the Australian Open. She had won the tournament in 1991, 1992, and 1993, and now, after a two-year absence, she was going for her fourth straight win. After rallying from a 5-2 third-set deficit against Chanda Rubin in the semifinals, she crushed Anke Huber 6-4, 6-1 for the title.

"I left this tournament in 1993 with unbelievable memories," she told the crowd after her victory. "To be back here holding this trophy means a lot to me." Just 22 years old, Monica could once again look forward to a future filled with limitless possibilities.

Whether the rest of the 1990s will belong to Monica Seles or another young star waiting in the wings remains to be seen. But women's tennis has already more than fulfilled the dreams of Billie Jean King. At the time of the King-Riggs match, the total prize money for women's tennis was less than $1 million per year. By the 1990s, the total had reached more than $24 million, and players could earn much more through exhibitions and endorsements. But more important than the money is the respect the players have earned. Now, young girls searching for role models can watch strong, talented women push themselves every day to be their best. The dedication and hard work of these tennis champions are an inspiration to all young women seeking to accomplish great things, whether on or off the tennis court.

SUGGESTIONS FOR FURTHER READING

Haney, Lynn. *Chris Evert, The Young Champion.* New York: G. P. Putnam's Sons, 1976.

Hilgers, Laura. *Steffi Graf.* New York: *Sports Illustrated For Kids* Books, 1990.

King, Billie Jean, with Frank Deford. *Billie Jean.* New York: Viking, 1982.

Kirkpatrick, Curry. *"Steppin' Out." Sports Illustrated,* May 27, 1991.

Knapp, Ron. *Sports Great Steffi Graf.* Springfield, NJ: Enslow Publishers, 1955.

Knudson, R. R. *Martina Navratilova, Tennis Power.* New York: Puffin, 1987.

Leder, Jane Mersky. *Martina Navratilova.* Mankato, MN: Crestwood House, 1985.

Lichtenstein, Grace. *A Long Way, Baby.* New York: William Morrow and Co., 1974.

Lloyd, Chris Evert, with Neil Amdur. *Chrissie, My Own Story.* New York: Simon and Schuster, 1982.

Mewshaw, Michael. *Ladies of the Court: Grace and Disgrace on the Women's Tennis Tour.* New York: Crown Publishers, Inc., 1993

Navratilova, Martina, with George Vecsey. *Martina.* New York: Alfred A. Knopf, 1985.

Price, S. L. *"The Return." Sports Illustrated,* July 17, 1995

Sanford, William R. and Carl R. Gree. *Billie Jean King.* New York: Macmillan Publishing Co., 1993.

INDEX

ABOUT THE AUTHOR

Martin Schwabacher is a writer and editor living in New York City. He grew up in Minneapolis, Minnesota, and attended Brown University. His other books for children include *The Chumash Indians*, *The Huron Indians*, and *Magic Johnson, Basketball Wizard.*

Picture Credits